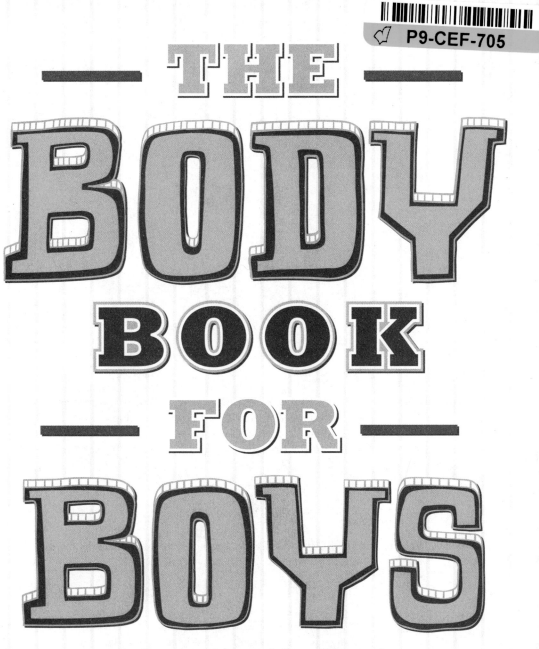

THE BODY BOOK FOR BOYS

By Jonathan Mar and Grace Norwich

Scholastic Inc.

New York   Toronto   London   Auckland   Sydney
Mexico City   New Delhi   Hong Kong

ISBN 978-0-545-23751-2

Copyright © 2010 by Scholastic Inc.

Published by Scholastic Inc. SCHOLASTIC and associated logos are trademarks and/or registered trademarks of Scholastic Inc.

12 11 10 9 8 7 6 5 4   13 14/0

Illustrated by Min Sung Ku
Designed by Angela Jun and Lissi Erwin
Printed in the U.S.A. 40
First printing, September 2010

This book is for informational purposes only and not intended as medical advice and should not replace the advice of or treatment by any health-care professional. You should consult your doctor with questions about your physical and mental well-being. This book should be considered a supplemental resource only.

CONTENTS

INTRODUCTION

From the moment we're born, our bodies and minds are constantly changing! Most of the time the **transformation** is so gradual that you hardly notice it. But then **puberty strikes**. All of a sudden, it seems to happen overnight. You wake up one morning, and it's as if a stranger is looking back at you in the mirror. Some developments are exciting (facial hair!). Others you'd just as soon live without, like that first bad breakout of acne right before class pics.

Puberty is full of ups and downs. During the low points, it's important to keep in mind that **you're not alone**! In fact, there are around ten million kids in the United States going through the same thing right now. Remember that the next time you feel like you're the only dude in the world whose voice cracks in the middle of math class! You have a lot of company while you're going through puberty. Sure, it can be **awkward** and frustrating at times but everything you're experiencing is completely normal.

Of course, just because **every other guy** in your grade is going through puberty doesn't always make the process any easier to handle. Along the way, you're bound to have questions that your classmates can't answer, and that you don't feel like bringing up at the dinner table with Mom or Dad. That's where **this guide** comes in. Think of it as someone who's been through puberty that can give you the 411 on **everything** that's going on with your body.

HOW TO GET THE MOST OUT OF THIS BOOK

You could find a spot to chill out and read this entire book cover to cover but remember—puberty doesn't happen that fast. It usually takes a few years to complete. For most guys, puberty starts between the ages of nine and fourteen. But that's just an average. **Every boy's body is different**, so some may start the process earlier, while some may start it later.

As you go through puberty, there may be a lot of months where you don't experience *any* changes. During those times you probably won't really need this book. But keep it in a safe place. Because all of a sudden—**wham!**—something totally unexpected will happen. It might be the appearance of hair where you once were bare. Or you might notice your voice changing. When this stuff happens, *The Body Book for Boys* will be there . . . ready when you need it.

The **main section** of the book is broken down by body part for quick reference. **Chapter 1** deals with everything above your shoulders, namely your head and neck. **Chapter 2** covers the upper body, including your shoulders, arms, and torso. **Chapter 3** addresses your private parts. **Chapter 4** deals with the lower body, right down to your legs and feet. Keep in mind that some aspects of puberty happen to more than one part of your body. For example, hair grows around your private parts, but also on your armpits. So it's covered in both places.

In a way, **Chapter 5** could be the most important chapter of all, because it deals with the stuff that happens on the inside during puberty. We're talking about the intense and often confusing emotions that are triggered as you transition from boy to man. Along with the **physical aspects of puberty**, these feelings are totally normal. But because you can't see them, they can be even harder to deal with. Just another reason to keep this book close by as a go-to resource during the awesome (and sometimes scary!) ride that is puberty.

WHEN TO EXPECT WHAT
(A TIMELINE)

This quick timeline will give you a sense of what's to come and in what order.

1

Stage One: Ages ten or younger

Most changes during this stage take place on the inside of your body through the release of hormones. You'll continue to get taller and heavier, but not at a rapid rate. You won't have any pubic hair yet.

2

Stage Two: Ages nine to fourteen

The first pubic hairs may start to come in around the base of the penis where it meets your body. Your testicles will start to get bigger and the skin of your scrotum will get thinner, looser, and darker in color.

3

Stage Three: Ages ten to fourteen

Most boys' voices start to get deeper. You'll probably begin your growth and weight spurts around this time, packing on the pounds and growing taller. Your shoulders may become broader and more muscular also. Your penis will start to get longer and darker in color. The first pubic hairs will become darker and curlier. They may start to spread to the scrotum.

4

Stage Four: Ages eleven to sixteen

You'll continue to get taller and heavier, and your first facial hair will come in. You'll probably notice other changes to your face too. The skin around the penis and scrotum will continue to get darker. The pubic hairs will now be dark, curly, and widespread.

5

Stage Five: Ages twelve to seventeen

The hair on your face will be thicker as well, possibly to the point where you can grow a beard, or at least some serious sideburns. Your penis and scrotum will be fully developed. Pubic hair will extend up to the belly and onto the thighs in a triangle pattern.

Although puberty happens throughout the entire body, **your head and neck** are super-busy during this time. For one thing, the brain is housed inside your head, and your brain controls the rest of your body. Some of these controls are **voluntary**, like walking and talking. Others are **involuntary**, like breathing or gland secretion (more on that in a sec). As for your neck, it contains the top of your spinal cord, which sends and receives information to and from the rest of your body through something called the central nervous system.

Then there's everything that's happening on the *outside of your head and neck*, starting with your face. As your eyes, nose, mouth, and other facial features develop, you start to lose your boyish appearance and **look more and more like a man**. Pretty cool, right? Unfortunately, the road to manhood is a bumpy one, and often those bumps appear on your face as zits and pimples. Ugh! Acne isn't the only concern you'll have to deal with during puberty. There's also **facial hair**, **oral hygiene**, and a funny little bump on your neck called the **Adam's apple**.

Cleansing Pads

ACNE 101

Every guy gets excited about his first scruffy beard. **No guy wants to deal with zits**. Unfortunately, acne is as inevitable to the whole puberty thing as facial hair. You might get lucky and only have to handle the occasional pimple. Or your face might break out into a constellation of blackheads and whiteheads. Either way, it's important to remember that **acne is totally normal**. In fact, studies show that nine out of ten kids experience it at one time or another during puberty. Acne may be a fact of life, but there are things you can do to prevent breakouts. Let's take a look at what causes acne to bust out in the first place.

WHERE DOES ACNE COME FROM?

Acne is a combination of overactive oil glands and clogged skin pores. Humans have oil glands all over their body, especially on the face, neck, chest, and back. Each gland is connected to a hair follicle. When the body is operating properly, oil from these glands flows up the hair follicle and out through pores in the skin. **This is how the body gets rid of dead skin cells**.

During **puberty**, your glands go into overdrive pumping out a lot more oil. As it does, dead skin cells start to clump up and block the pores. When this happens, the oil that normally flows out the pore gets trapped beneath it. The result? A tiny white bump beneath the skin's surface, called a whitehead.

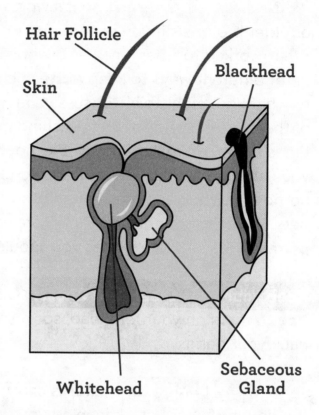

Hair Follicle

Blackhead

Skin

Whitehead

Sebaceous Gland

As the **pressure** builds, the trapped oil starts to push up the skin's surface. When bacteria on the skin gets into the trapped oil, the infection causes redness and swelling. The result is a pimple, also known as a zit. If the infection gets bad enough, bacteria will spread beneath the skin to other parts of the body, igniting a full-blown case of acne all over the face, neck, chest, and back.

BATTLING THE BLACKHEADS

Acne runs in the fam, so it's worth talking to a parent or older bro or sis if you're suffering from a major outbreak. What worked for them may also work for you. There are a lot of different ways to keep **acne** in check. And contrary to what you might think, obsessive face washing *isn't* one of them. As a matter of fact, washing more than a few times a day can make acne *worse*, not better, especially if you use super-abrasive soaps and scrubs. The other big no-no is popping a pimple, no matter how big and juicy it gets. Popping not only leads to more acne, it might leave a permanent scar. Here's what you should do instead:

Keep Your Hair Clean and Short: Oily hair can cause **breakouts** on your forehead, so wash it often and trim back your bangs.

Consider Creams: Drug stores carry a lot of "over-the-counter" products (meaning you don't need a doc's prescription to buy them) designed to treat acne. Most contain **benzoyl peroxide**, which **kills** the bacteria that causes pimples and also unclogs pores. Be sure to read the instructions closely, and go easy in the beginning, since benzoyl peroxide causes allergies and **skin irritations** in some people. Products that contain **salicylic acid** can also be effective, especially for milder cases of acne.

Consult a Physician: If your acne is too severe for over-the-counter treatment, or if most of your pimples are red, under the skin, and without any whiteheads, talk with an adult about seeing a dermatologist. This is a **doctor** who specializes in skin conditions. He or she will be able to prescribe a stronger medication that may be better at fighting your particular type of acne.

Eat Right: A lot of people think things like candy and greasy food cause acne. There's actually not much proof of that, although too much fast food or sweets can lead to other health issues. When it comes to acne, doctors do **recommend** certain nutrients, including zinc, which is found in nuts and seeds, and vitamin A, which is found in carrots, broccoli, and other vegetables.

STRAIGHT TALK

You wake up one morning, look in the mirror, and staring back at you is an enormous zit, right on the tip of your nose! Or a **road map** of pimples across your forehead! You may be tempted to make a huge production of the acne at school. But making comments and jokes about it will only draw more attention. If you pretend the pimples aren't there, chances are everyone else will, too (you are definitely more aware of them than anyone else). And don't go for the Band-Aid-over-the-pimple trick. It will only lead to more looks.

REAL GUYS USE LOTION

No, it's not just for girls. Lots of guys use lotion to prevent dry, itchy skin, or to make their faces soft and smooth. But hey, we understand if you don't want to share this particular hygiene habit with the world. Fortunately, there are lots of lotions that are fragrance-free, so you won't have to worry about leaving a scent as you walk down the halls at school. Just remember to rub it in all the way! The best time to apply lotion is when you get out of the shower, since it will be able to penetrate your open skin pores.

A WORD OF WARNING ABOUT TANNING

You might like **the bronzed surfer look** that a few hours under the hot sun gives you. But you can really pay for it in the long run. In fact, the American Academy of Dermatology warns that even a single case of **severe sunburn** when you're young can double your lifetime risk of **melanoma**, a serious form of skin cancer. Even if you avoid that, too much fun in the sun will increase your chances of turning **wrinkly** when you're older.

This doesn't mean you should never set foot in the sunlight again. But you should **always wear sunscreen** when you'll be under the sun for any extended period of time, especially between 10 A.M. and 4 P.M., when the rays are at their hottest. Experts recommend slathering on lotion with an SPF (short for "sun protection factor") of 30 or above. Remember to reapply the lotion frequently, say every two hours, especially after taking dips in the pool or ocean. And don't forget the tops of your ears and other easy-to-forget places!

THE DOS AND DON'TS OF HAIR CARE

Boys have it a lot easier than girls when it comes to maintaining their hair. Unless you decide to become a rock star or pro wrestler, chances are you'll keep your 'do pretty short. But, you still have to take care of your hair to keep it healthy and looking good.

Proper hair care is super-important during puberty, since your body's **sebaceous glands** are pumping out more oil than ever. This oil is designed to keep your hair shiny and protect it from water damage. (If you've ever seen oil from a car in a puddle of water, you know that the two liquids don't mix.) A little bit of oil is good for hair. But too much can leave it looking greasy. Even if you never had this problem as a kid, now that you're entering **puberty**, you'll start to notice that your hair has a little extra shine to it.

Fortunately, it's pretty easy to prevent hair from becoming greasy. The most important thing is to **wash regularly in the shower**. Depending on how much oil your body produces, as well as how much you sweat during sports and exercise, you may need to shampoo once a day. Some people get away with shampooing every other day, or even just a couple times a week.

A gentle shampoo is best for most hair types. If you've been washing regularly and your hair still feels super-slick, you might want to experiment with shampoos that are specially formulated for **oily hair**. There's also conditioner, which is designed to take the tangles out of long or curly hair. A lot of guys use conditioner, but if your problem is greasy hair you probably shouldn't since it may contain a lot of oil.

DID YOU KNOW?

The human head is covered with more than one hundred thousand hairs. Anywhere between fifty and one hundred hairs fall out every day while you're showering, combing, and brushing—or even just eating lunch! The average life span of a human hair is two to six years, at which time it falls out and is replaced by a new hair from the same follicle.

TO GEL OR NOT TO GEL?

Some guys use **gels** or **molds** to help style their hair. You might want to stay away from wax-based ones in the beginning since they're tougher to wash out. And if you can come up with a 'do that works for you *without* the need for additional products, even better. Not only do gels and molds cost money, you have to worry about taking them everywhere you go.

THE FACTS ABOUT FACIAL HAIR

Of all the things that **happen** during puberty, facial hair is probably the coolest. It opens up a whole new world of possibilities, from the trim goatees worn by many actors to the rugged five o'clock shadows favored by big-time athletes.

Facial hair usually arrives a little later in the puberty process, after hair has started to grow around your private parts and armpits. On average, boys are between the ages of fourteen and sixteen when the first facial hairs appear, typically around the corners of their upper lip. At first, these hairs are often light in color and soft in texture. As the hairs spread across the lip, they become darker, thicker, and coarser. After the **moustache** fills out, facial hair usually spreads to the cheeks, chin, sideburns, and upper neck.

By the time they're **eighteen**, a lot of guys are able to sport a full beard. But others are into their twenties before their facial hair has developed completely. And for some, facial hair never grows beyond a few whiskers.

19

HOW-TO:

THE ART OF SHAVING

Regardless of how thick your facial hair is, you definitely want to become familiar with a razor. Just don't expect shaving to make your facial hair grow back thicker. This is a common myth, but it's not actually true. Hair may look thicker, but that's just because you've shaved off the thin tips.

Some men start each day with a shave, while others only shave every few days. Even those who wear a beard or moustache shave around the edges to keep things stylin'. No matter what kind of look you go for, the steps for shaving are always similar. **Here they are in order:**

1) Step One: Choose your razor

Buying your first razor is **definitely exciting**. Most guys go with a **blade razor**. **Electric shavers** are an option if you're worried about cutting yourself. Electric shavers don't require shaving cream, so they're handy for men who do a lot of traveling. But they don't deliver as close a shave.

If you go for a blade razor, you'll find **disposable** types and those that use cartridge razors. **Cartridges** tend to deliver the smoothest shave, especially if you choose a multi-blade razor. No matter what type of blade you choose, it's important to keep it clean and sharp. A dull blade can cause nicks and cuts to your face, as well as a painful rash known as **razor burn**. Ouch!

2) Step Two: Prep your skin

Always start by wetting your face with warm water. Then apply a shaving cream or gel to soften the hair and lubricate the skin. **Never use regular bar soap**, which hardens hair and dulls the blade. And don't even *think* about shaving your dry face, unless you want to leave a mean case of razor burn that'll hang around all day.

3) Step Three: Shave away

Once your face is lathered up, you're ready to shave. Over most of your face, including your upper lip, it's best to shave downward in the direction of the hair growth. Don't apply too much pressure. The razor will do the work, as you rinse often in warm water to keep the blades free of hair. Some men switch to an **upward direction** under their chin and along the neck to give these areas a close shave. However, the upward motion increases the risk of razor bumps.

4) Step Four: Cool down

Finish every shave by rinsing your face with **cool water** to help close the pores and soothe your skin. Then pat your face dry with a soft towel. If you have sensitive skin, consider applying an alcohol-free shaving lotion.

OPEN WIDE

THE SECRET TO FRESH BREATH AND PEARLY WHITES

Your mouth doesn't change much during puberty. But now is the time to develop good habits around mouth care, otherwise known as oral hygiene. These routines will keep your teeth strong and your smile bright for a lifetime. They'll also prevent bad breath. Ask any girl, and she'll tell you that a nice smile and good breath are two features important in a guy. **Here's how to get them:**

Brush Regularly: Dentists say that you need to **brush** your teeth for at least two minutes twice a day to remove plaque, a clear bacteria that coats the teeth and causes cavities and decay. Choose a brush with **soft bristles** and don't apply too much pressure, since this can harm the gums. Start with the outside surface of the teeth, brushing a few teeth at a time using small strokes.

Chewing **sugar-free gum** can help mask bad breath, especially after midday meals when you might not have time to brush.

Chewing Gum Sugar Free

Then move to the insides and tops of the teeth, before finishing up with the tongue. That's right, you need to brush your tongue to get rid of the bacteria that cause bad breath.

Don't Forget to Floss: Most people remember to brush their teeth. Flossing is a way harder habit to get into, but it's just as important to maintaining healthy teeth and gums. Dentists recommend flossing once a day, **ideally after your last meal of the day**. The goal is to remove food bits, as well as plaque, from between the teeth. Insert the floss between two teeth and gently bring it to the gum line. Curve the floss around each tooth and slide it up and down.

Go for Checkups: **Regular** brushing and flossing are the first steps toward healthy teeth. But you also need to visit the dentist **every six months** for a checkup and cleaning. Nobody likes going to the dentist, but it's a lot less unpleasant than a mouthful of rotting teeth.

BRACING FOR BRACES

You can brush and floss religiously and **visit the dentist** every six months like clockwork, but your teeth still might end up growing in crooked. This starts to happen when the adult teeth first come in, around the age of six or seven, but dentists usually don't refer patients to an **orthodontist** for braces until they're in their teens. That's lousy timing, given everything else that's going on with your body. But in most cases, braces only have to stay on for between six months and a couple of years. If you can't stand the thought of being a metal mouth, ask your orthodontist about braces made out of clear ceramic. There are also **"invisible braces"** that attach to the inside of the teeth.

DID YOU KNOW?

Your tongue is covered with about ten thousand tiny nerve endings called **taste buds.** These taste buds respond to different tastes, including salty, sweet, savory, sour, and bitter. When you eat ice cream, the sweet nerve endings send a signal to the brain. When you eat peanuts, the salty nerve endings send the message.

WHAT'S THAT

YOU SAY?

Ears aren't much to look at, but they're one of the body's finest instruments. Not only does the ear **receive sound** and send it to the brain, it also helps with **coordination** by maintaining your body's balance. Who knew that taking good care of your ears could help you make that catch in the outfield?

You may have heard the rule about not sticking anything smaller than your elbow into your ear. Well, it's true. And it goes for **cotton swabs**, even though a bunch of people think of them as earwax removers (including a lot of adults who should really know better!). In fact, earwax is good for you, since the sticky stuff prevents dirt from getting too deep into the ear canal, where it can cause infections. Regular scrubbing in the shower should be enough to keep the outside of your ears clean.

The other thing to remember about your ears is that they can be **damaged** by loud noise, including **music from your headphones**. The rule of thumb is that if other people can hear what you're listening to on your headphones, it's time to dial it down. You might think, *I listen to a ton of loud music on my headphones and I can hear fine.* But over time, this excessive volume can lead to ringing in the ears, dizziness, and even permanent hearing loss.

EYES:
A CLOSER LOOK

If you're reading this book, congrats! It means you have at least one **good eye**, and probably a pair of them. Doctors use eye charts to determine a person's **visual acuity**, or ability to see. **Chances** are you've already had this examination, so you should know what kind of vision you have; 20/20 is considered perfect, and means you can see clearly at twenty feet what a normal eye can see at twenty feet. If you have 15/20 vision, you have to be **five feet closer** to see clearly. Make's sense, right?

Nothing about puberty should **affect your vision**. No hormones change the way your eye receives information or sends it to your brain. But, as your body ages, the eyes age too. So even if you're 20/20 today, your eyesight may start to change at some point. About thirty percent of Americans are nearsighted, meaning they can see objects that are close by, like the print in a book, but not those that are far away, like an airplane in the sky. About sixty percent of them are farsighted; they can see objects fine from a distance, but not those that are close at hand.

Nearsightedness and **farsightedness** can be corrected with eyeglasses or contact lenses, both of which help the eye to focus light in the appropriate spot. **Glasses** are easier to put on and take off, plus they come in a lot of styles. **Contacts** are invisible, but they can be harder to use.

E — 1
F M — 2
T N X — 3
I L W R — 4
Y J G H O — 5
K C U A P B — 6
E D Q M O N F — 7

PUT ON PROTECTIVE GOGGLES IN HIGH-RISK SITUATIONS.

That goes for sports with flying objects, lacrosse, or hockey. It also applies to science lab, where chemicals can spray into the eye, or shop class, where flying wood chips pose a similar threat.

WEAR SUNGLASSES.

Excessive light can damage your eyes and cause cataracts, which cloud a person's vision by preventing light from reaching the retina. Sunglasses keep too much light from getting through to the eye—and they have the added benefit of looking pretty stylin'.

FRAME GAMES

The best thing about wearing glasses (besides the fact that they'll help you see straight!) is picking out the frames. Leaf through a couple of men's fashion magazines and you'll get a sense of how many varieties there are to choose from, and how they each create a different look—chill, sophisticated, geek-cool, you name it.

Of course, all those options can make picking the right frames a serious headache. **Fortunately**, the shape of your face is a great guide for which shape frame is best.

ROUND FACE: Contrast the shape of your face with a boxy, rectangular frame.

SQUARE FACE: Go with a simple oval frame to soften the hard edges of your jawline and jutting chin.

OVAL FACE: Large glasses with rounded-square frames will balance your features. Stay away from angles, since they'll look too hard against your face.

WHAT THE NECK?

You probably never paid much attention to your neck before. But during puberty, it's the scene of a pretty major event: **voice change**. Most boys' voices start to get deeper between the ages of twelve and fourteen, toward the end of the puberty process.

This drop in octave has to do with the **larynx** (or voice box), which is located inside your throat. You can find yours by touching the front of your throat as you hum. Anytime you speak, air from your lungs causes the vocal cords that stretch across your larynx to vibrate, producing the sound of your voice.

Remember what you sounded like as a kid? **Vocal cords** are small and thin on young boys, which is why their voices are high-pitched. During puberty, the release of testosterone into the body causes the larynx to grow. As it gets bigger, the vocal cords that stretch across it get longer and thicker. From start to finish, a boy's vocal cords might get up to **sixty percent** longer during puberty! As the cords grow, the sound produced by their vibrations gets deeper and deeper.

The process usually happens slowly, so much so that you may not even notice your voice becoming deeper. As your larynx and vocal cords adjust, you might experience the occasional **crack**. Hopefully, this won't happen in the middle of English class. But if it does, try not to worry too much about it. You weren't the first and you definitely won't be the last. After a few months your larynx and vocal cords will settle down, and your voice won't make any more sudden **squeaks**.

THE ORIGIN OF THE
ADAM'S APPLE

For some guys, their larynx gets so big during puberty that it starts to stick out at the front of the throat. You might notice this bulge bobbing up and down when your dad or older relative takes a drink. The bump gets its name from the bible story of **Adam and Eve** in the Garden of Eden. After Adam ate the forbidden apple, a piece of the fruit became lodged in his throat. The enlarged larynx that some men have is said to resemble the small, rounded apple in Adam's throat. Girls also have a larynx that gets bigger during puberty, but not nearly as big as a boy's. This is why a woman's voice doesn't get as deep as a man's.

GET YOUR HEAD IN THE GAME WITH THIS POP QUIZ

1. Which of the following is NOT recommended for acne treatment?

A) Washing your face ten times a day

B) Popping pimples at the first sign

C) Getting a doc's script before you have a major outbreak

D) All of the above

2. True or False

Shaving will help your facial hair come in faster.

3. Vocal cords grow by what percentage during puberty?

    A) 10 percent

    B) 40 percent

    C) 60 percent

    D) 200 percent

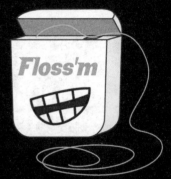

4. The best time to floss your teeth is:

    A) Once a year on your birthday

    B) Right after your last meal

    C) Before you go to bed

    D) When you go to the dentist

5. The Adam's apple is named after:

    A) Adam Sandler

    B) Adam of Adam and Eve

    C) John Adams

    D) John Quincy Adams

Answers:
1. D
2. False. There's no way to speed up the growth of facial hair.
3. C
4. B
5. B

THE LOWDOWN ON THE UPPER BODY

Your upper body may not seem like the scene of much change during puberty. But in fact, there's as much going on between your neck and waistline as anywhere else on the body. For one thing, **the upper body** is home to a ton of vital organs, including the heart, lungs, and stomach. The habits you develop now will impact the development of these organs, and determine your overall health for years to come.

Start smoking, for example, and your heart and lungs could be damaged forever. Eat too much junk food, and your stomach will grow to an unhealthy size. The upper body also contains some of the **largest muscles** in the body. As these muscles start to develop at a rapid pace, the shape and proportion of your body will change. Then there are the armpits, which are responsible for one of puberty's least pleasant transformations—**body odor**.

BASIC BODY TYPES

As your body **develops**, you'll become more aware of its size, shape, and proportion. You'll probably also notice that not all guys' bodies look the same. Some are tall and lean. Some are short and round. And some are in between. You know, **diet and exercise** have a lot to do with the shape of a person's body. But it's also true that the male body comes in three basic types: ectomorph, endomorph, and mesomorph. Here's a quick description of each—and no matter what kind of type you have, appreciate it!

ECTOMORPHS tend to be long, tall, and lean, with narrow shoulders, flat chests, and less muscle mass than other body types.

ENDOMORPHS are rounder and softer in the middle. They have more body fat than other types, often concentrated in the belly (or at least that's often how it appears) and relatively short arms and legs.

MESOMORPHS are usually the most muscular body type, with broad shoulders, a tapered torso, and a relatively narrow waist. Their arms and legs tend to be long and well developed.

BOOSTING BODY CONFIDENCE

Let's face it. We live in a world that's obsessed with body image. In movies and mags, the ideal man is usually tall and muscular. But if you look again at the **three main body types**, you see that that type of body is not very common. Men can be tall (**ectomorph**) and they can be muscular (**mesomorph**), but **to be both qualities at the same time is pretty unusual**. Our point? Don't get too hung up comparing your body with others, especially those from the airbrushed, smoke-and-mirrors world of magazines and movies.

Keep in mind that everyone's body is a little out of whack during the middle and high school years. The secret is to focus on the features of your body that you like and don't worry about the rest. The **right outfit** can make the difference. For example, have lean, muscular legs from playing lots of soccer? Don't be afraid to show them off in the warmer months by wearing shorts! If, on the other hand, you're on the shorter side, wearing shirts with vertical stripes will make you appear taller.

MIGHTY MUSCLES

Your body will definitely change shape as you go through puberty. This will be especially obvious in your upper body, since it contains some of the **biggest muscle groups**. Did you know there are more than six hundred muscles in the human body? During puberty, the release of **testosterone** into the body causes all of these muscles to grow. This is sometimes referred to as the **strength spurt**, since it makes muscles bigger and stronger.

Girls don't have as much testosterone in their bodies, so they don't develop muscles the same way boys do. **But they can still be pretty tough**!

Some muscles grow more than others during the **strength spurt**. Those in the upper body are particularly active. The shoulder muscles, also known as the **deltoids**, get broader, as do the chest muscles, also known as the **pectoralis majors**. As the muscles of the upper body broaden, the hips start to seem narrower by comparison. This will be especially apparent in mesomorphs (the most muscular body type), but all guys who take care of their bodies will experience this upside-down-triangle effect. It's what distinguishes a boy's body from that of a man.

STRAIGHT TALK

You like a girl at school, but she only seems interested in star athletes with big muscles. Unfortunately, you're more of the studious type. Do you pursue her anyway? Probably not. If a girl is only interested in a guy's body, chances are she's not that interesting on the inside. You're better off finding someone who shares your interests and passions.

THE DOS AND DON'TS OF BODY BUILDING

It's **human nature** to want a strong, healthy body, especially if you happen to be a guy. Our society definitely rewards strength and fitness, whether it's by handing out multimillion-dollar contracts to the best athletes in a sport, or by casting tall, strong guys as the leading men in Hollywood movies.

But it's important to **be patient** with your body's strength spurt, and recognize that not every guy has bulging muscles and a washboard stomach (in fact, only a tiny percentage of men have this physique). The best thing you can do to **maximize your body's potential** is lead an active life. Any physical activity, such as riding your bike or playing soccer, will make your muscles stronger.

Weight training can also help build muscles, but only if you do it later in puberty when your body is making enough testosterone. As a general rule, you probably shouldn't be pumping iron before you've started shaving. And when you *do* start lifting weights, make sure you do it under the **supervision of a coach or trainer**. Otherwise, you run the risk of injuring yourself or even stunting your body's growth.

STAY OFF THE STEROIDS

You've probably heard about drugs that make the body stronger. **Steroids** are a class of hormone originally developed to help people fight cancer and other deadly diseases. But some athletes and weight lifters use (or it would be more accurate to say, "abuse") these **strength-enhancing narcotics**. Here are five reasons why you shouldn't even think about doing the same:

- Steroids stunt the body's growth, especially if taken during puberty.
- Performance-enhancing drugs are illegal in sports. Just ask the many athletes who have been suspended or had their reputations tarnished by taking steroids.
- Steroids can cause your testicles to shrink and your breasts to get larger.
- Over time, steroids can result in serious health risks, such as liver damage and heart attacks.
- Steroids lead to all sorts of mental health issues, including moodiness and violent outbursts, aka "roid rage."

BODY ODOR: IT'S THE PITS!

hen you're a kid, sweat is no big deal. Sure, your shirt gets a little damp after a day out under the hot summer sun. But otherwise, sweat is, well, nothing to sweat about. In fact, sweat is the body's **built-in cooling system**. There are millions of sweat glands covering the entire surface of your body. When the temperature rises or you run around a lot, these glands release moisture onto the skin through your **pores**. Sweat is ninety-nine percent water and a small amount of salt, sugar, and natural chemicals. As this sweat evaporates from your skin, it cools down the body. The salt in sweat causes the body to produce more of the stuff, which keeps the cycle going.

Then puberty strikes. All of a sudden, sweat doesn't just cool you off. It also stinks. Remember those sweat glands that are located all over the body? Well, the ones in your **armpits** become active for the first time during puberty. Bacteria that live on the skin love the sweat from these glands. They all flock there. Not only do **bacteria** like the taste of sweat from your underarm glands, the moist, warm conditions are perfect for breeding. As a result, they end up making themselves at home and staying a while. Eventually, as the bacteria break down more sweat, they start to give off a gross smell. This smell is also known as **body odor**.

TAKING THE "PU" OUT OF PUBERTY

You may not notice your body odor right away, but chances are those around you will. Hopefully one of your friends or family members will tip you off before the **cute girl** you have a crush on in social studies does! Either way, it's time to start **paying attention** to your body odor.

Bathing regularly is the first line of defense. Duh! Remember to lather up with soap, since you need to fight back the bacteria that cause odor. **If you don't like to shower in the mornings**, jump in before you go to bed.

This is just as effective at preventing odor, plus the hot water will **relax** your body and help you get a good night's sleep. Showering at night will also save you a few extra minutes in the morning.

Deodorant is the second line of defense. Drugstores and supermarkets have entire aisles filled with different types of deodorant. But deciding which one is right for you can be a little tricky. In the beginning, it's best to **avoid anything with "antiperspirant"** on their label. These products contain chemicals that actually block the sweat glands. Adults who sweat a lot need to use antiperspirants.

But you don't want to mess with your glands when they're just starting to work for the first time. Go with a straight deodorant instead, finding one with a scent you like, or use unscented.

CAN GUYS REALLY GROW BREASTS?

Breast development isn't just for girls. Approximately **fifty percent** of boys experience swelling under their nipples during puberty, often to the point where it looks like they're growing breasts. The swelling often comes with soreness and tenderness, and some boys develop hard, round **bumps** under one or both nipples.

The medical term for male breasts is **gynecomastia**, and it's a perfectly **normal** reaction to hormones. Of course, the fact that it's normal doesn't make it any easier to deal with. Unfortunately, there's no way to treat the swelling, but it will go away on its own in a matter of months. So in the meantime, throw on a baggy shirt and try to forget about it.

MAKING THE MOST OUT OF MAJOR ORGANS

Every human organ is vital, but none more than the **heart** and **lungs**. They're what keep blood, nutrients, and oxygen pumping throughout your bod. During puberty, these organs are **working overtime** as you grow and get stronger. That's why it's super-important to keep your heart and lungs in top shape. **Here are three ways:**

Don't smoke. Guys who smoke have a seventy percent higher death rate! That's because more than **four thousand substances** have been found in cigarette smoke. The worst of them is probably **carbon monoxide**, which prevents the blood from carrying the max amount of oxygen through your body. Carbon monoxide also damages the heart and blood vessels.

Get plenty of exercise. It's not just your **muscles** that benefit when you put in extra hours on the basketball court.

Your lungs need exercise to become strong enough to supply your body with the oxygen it needs. Sports, outdoor activities, and just walking briskly give your **heart** a workout, too, enabling it to pump blood and nutrients to every part of your bod.

Maintain a healthy diet.
Try to eat five servings of **fruits and veggies** a day. Snack on apples, celery sticks, or raisins. Stay away from soda and junk food. It's tough, but everything in moderation. Also, wait a few minutes before you go back for seconds to make sure you're really hungry.

49

TORSO TIPS

The midsection of your body contains a lot of important **organs**, including your stomach, intestines, liver, kidneys, and more. As you go through puberty, these organs **develop rapidly** as part of the body's weight spurt. The weight spurt is related to the more familiar growth spurt (more details in Chapter 4). Both spurts last an average of **three to four years**. A boy might pack on twenty pounds or more in a single year during this time. From start to finish, the average weight gain is about **fifty pounds**!

That's a lot of **extra weight** in a short amount of time. But if you eat well and exercise, the pounds should be distributed evenly around your body. **Bigger muscles and bones** will account for a large percentage of the weight gain. If you eat too much junk food or spend hours in front of the TV or on the computer, you might notice that your **stomach** is growing faster than the rest of your body.

Unfortunately, this is the case with a lot of teens and tweens. According to the Centers for Disease Control, nearly fifteen percent of kids between the ages of six to eleven were overweight. Doctors have even started referring to the **"obesity epidemic"** among kids. A person is considered obese if he weighs twenty percent more than his ideal weight.

Weighing too much can lead to all sorts of health problems like high **cholesterol** and **high blood pressure**. It can also cause a condition called sleep apnea, which keeps you from getting a good night's sleep during the time when your body needs it the most. **Maybe worst of all**, being overweight can lead to depression and low self-esteem. Being a teenager is one of the most exciting and challenging times of your life. You definitely want to be in top physical shape to make the most of it.

WHAT'S YOUR IDEAL WEIGHT?

So how do you know what the right weight is for you? As you saw, you're going to pack on a lot of **pounds** at a rapid rate during puberty. **But how much is too much**? Doctors use something called the body mass index, or **BMI** for short, to determine a person's ideal weight. You should know that the ideal BMI is different for teens than it is for adults. Next time you go to the doc for a checkup, ask him or her to **measure** your BMI. Or you can go onto the

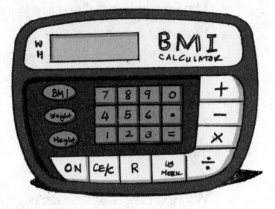

Internet and search for a BMI calculator. Ask a parent or other adult to help you plug in the data, since it can be a little complicated. BMI calculators aren't perfect, but they're a good way to figure out if your weight is in the right ballpark.

WATCHING YOUR WEIGHT

If it turns out you are heavier than you should be, the first thing you should do is **talk to a trusted adult** about the issue. This may be your mom or dad, coach, or a favorite teacher at school. Weight is a pretty **sensitive** subject, so it can be hard to talk about. Try not to worry too much or be embarrassed. Fact of the matter is, most people **worry** about their weight at one time or another. Being **out in the open** about how you feel is the best way to fix the problem.

Losing weight is usually a matter of **eating right** and **getting enough exercise**. Easier said than done, especially if other members of your family aren't doing it. If that's the case, see if you can convince your fam to go on a **health kick** with you. Even a few small changes can make a difference. For example, exercising ten minutes a day a few times a week and **cutting out soda** from your diet is a great start. Sometimes weight loss is more complicated than just diet and exercise, and can be affected by **genetics** (what your 'rents hand down to you). You should consult a doctor or nutritionist before starting on any serious weight-loss program.

SUPER SUBS

Everybody loves fast food and sweets. Unfortunately, that stuff is loaded with fat, salt, sugar, and calories, none of which make for a very healthy diet. We're not saying you can never eat at a fast food restaurant again, but if that's what you really want, try to save it for special occasions, like your b-day, or to celebrate a great report card. Fortunately, there are plenty of things that taste just as good. **Here are a few substitutes** for your fave foods that are sure to satisfy!

AT A BBQ

Instead of a...
cheeseburger
Fat: 26 g
Calories: 570
Sodium: 1,190 mg

Try the...
beef kabob
Fat: 4 g
Calories: 140
Sodium: 470 mg

AT THE MOVIES

Instead of a...
popcorn
Fat: 31 g
Calories: 664
Sodium: 1,143 mg

Try the...
soft pretzel
Fat: 3 g
Calories: 160
Sodium: 130 mg

AT BREAKFAST

Instead of a...bowl of sugary cereal
Fat: 0.6 g
Calories: 118
Sugar: 312.5 g

Try the...bowl of whole grain cereal
Fat: .7 g
Calories: 113
Sugar: 1.15 g

EXCUSE BUSTERS

Think you have a good reason not to exercise?

We've heard 'em all! And short of broken bones, not one is good enough.

I'm way too tired. You won't be after a few weeks of regular exercise. Believe it or not, the **more energy** you expend, the more you produce.

I'm too busy. Oh yeah? You don't have **ten minutes** in the morning and ten after school? Because that's all it takes. And you know you spend that much time on Facebook.

I'm the perfect weight already. That may be true, but exercise is about more than weight control. It's also about building **strength**, **stamina**, and **self-confidence**.

I'm not athletic. Nobody said you have to become captain of the lacrosse team. **Hiking**, **biking**, and even **walking** are enough to get the heart pumping.

GIVE YOURSELF A HAND
(AND AN ARM)

The arms and hands sometimes grow faster than the torso during puberty. This can make some teenage boys' bodies look a little **gorilla-like**, with their long arms and big hands swinging down beneath their waists. But—phew!—**everything evens out** once their torso has a chance to catch up. As the arms and hands grow, they'll also become more muscular and hairy.

Your hands help you experience the world through the sensation of touch. That's why it's important to take really good care of your hands, for example by wearing **protective gloves** and wrist guards when playing contact sports or working with tools.

It's also a **good idea** to keep your hands and nails clean. This will prevent the spread of germs and also make a positive impression when you meet people for the first time. If you're a nail-biter, switch to a **nail clipper** right

away. Not only does nail biting look gross in public, you're practically inviting germs and bacteria into your body.

GET THE UPPER HAND WITH THIS POP QUIZ

1. A person is considered obese if they're overweight by what percentage?

    A) 10 percent

    B) 20 percent

    C) 50 percent

    D) 100 percent

2. True or False

    Steroid use is okay if you only use them moderately.

3. The human body has how many muscles?

    A) 100

    B) 200

    C) 300

    D) 600

4. Boys put on an average of how many pounds during puberty?

    A) 10 pounds

    B) 25 pounds

    C) 50 pounds

    D) 100 pounds

5. President Barack Obama has the following body type:

    A) Mesomorph

    B) Ectomorph

    C) Endomorph

    D) None of the above

Answers:

1. B

2. False. Any level of steroid use can cause serious side effects.

3. D

4. C

5. B

Of all the changes that happen during puberty, the ones discussed in this chapter are probably the most **mysterious**. After all, these are your private parts we're talking about. If everything down there were hanging out in the open, guys your age wouldn't have nearly so many questions. But we don't live in a nudist society (thank goodness). As a result, boys entering puberty have **all sorts of concerns** about the size and shape of their penis, not to mention the new set of urges and emotions that seem to be emanating from that part of your bod. We'll get to all of these issues, but first, you need to know a few basics about anatomy.

WHAT TO EXPECT DOWN THERE

DURING PUBERTY

Just as your body goes through a growth spurt during puberty, so does your penis. For some boys, this process starts as early as the age of nine. For others, it doesn't begin until they're fourteen or fifteen. In most cases, the process takes **three to four years** to complete, but this, too, can vary. Puberty patterns usually run in the fam, so you can ask your dad, big bro, or other older male relative when they started to notice changes, and how long the process took. Of course, they may not remember exact dates. That's why it's always **best not to make too many comparisons**, and just let your body develop at its own rate.

MALE SEX ORGAN

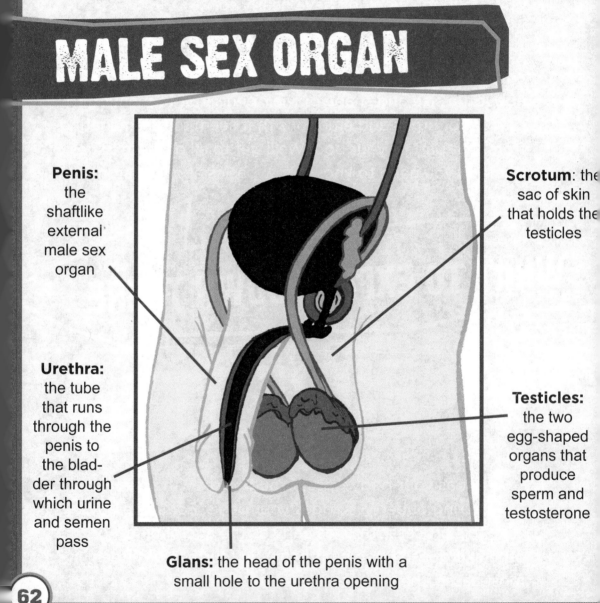

Penis: the shaftlike external male sex organ

Urethra: the tube that runs through the penis to the bladder through which urine and semen pass

Scrotum: the sac of skin that holds the testicles

Testicles: the two egg-shaped organs that produce sperm and testosterone

Glans: the head of the penis with a small hole to the urethra opening

Your scrotum and testicles will be the first to show signs of change during puberty. As the scrotum gets longer, the testicles get bigger and hang lower. The skin around your scrotum will also start to become darker and looser. These changes are pretty subtle and gradual, so you may not even notice them at first. In fact, doctors need a special tool called an **orchidometer**, 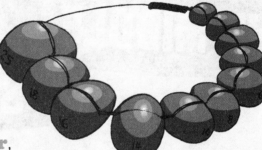 which looks like a string of plastic or wooden beads, to measure testicle size. So don't be alarmed if your doctor pulls this tool out during your next checkup!

Around the time the testicles begin **growing**, the first **pubic hair** starts to come in. This is usually the first visible sign that changes are happening "down there." You might develop small bumps on your skin in the area where the penis meets the body. Pubic hairs poking through the surface of the skin are the reason for these bumps. In the beginning, pubic hair is soft, like the hair that grows on your stomach.

Little dots on the scrotum and penis are also common (and perfectly normal) during the early stage. These are oil and sweat glands, similar to the ones that develop on other parts of the body during puberty. They don't result in acne (like those on the face) or body odor (like those in the armpits), but the skin around your **private parts** might feel moist and give off a different scent.

THE MIDDLE STAGES

After the testicles and pubic hair begin their growth spurt, the penis starts to grow longer. The skin on the penis and scrotum continues to become darker and looser, and the testicles keep getting bigger. As the testicles grow, you might start to notice that one is bigger than the other. This is common and it's normally the right testicle that's bigger than the left. (Weird but true!) During the **middle stage**, pubic hair will begin to come in a little thicker. Unlike the first hairs, these hairs will be curlier, coarser, and darker, and also start to spread beyond the initial patch around the base of the penis.

END GAINS

Before, the penis was just getting longer. Now it's getting wider, too. Boys are usually around thirteen when they start this final stage of genital development. **Over the next few years**, the penis and testicles will continue to grow and the skin will keep getting darker. Pubic hair will fill in as well, spreading up toward the belly and out onto the thighs in a triangle pattern. The hair becomes so bushy on some men that they choose to trim it with scissors, just like the hair on their head.

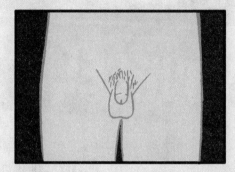

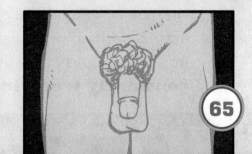

PROTECTING
YOURSELF "DOWN THERE"

You only have to get hit in the testicles once to know how **painful** it can be. Sometimes the pain is intense enough to cause vomiting. Fortunately, it usually goes away after a few minutes. All you can really do is walk it off and wait. A **jockstrap** and **cup** can prevent future injuries. A cup is a hard piece of triangular plastic that slips into the jockstrap to protect your genital area. It's required in physical sports, since a severe blow to the testicles can cause permanent damage (but don't freak out—permanent damage is *very* rare).

DOES SIZE MATTER?

No matter what stage of development they're in, **penis size** is definitely one of the most persistent male hang-ups. Some guys carry the issue all the way into adulthood, **constantly worrying** that the size of their penis somehow makes them less of a man. The fact of the matter is, size has nothing to do with masculinity. First of all, there isn't any connection between penis size and body strength. Your penis doesn't affect things like balance and hand-eye coordination, and a big penis won't make you any more or less brave. It definitely doesn't have anything to do with whether or not girls will like you.

WHAT'S THE AVERAGE SIZE?

Still looking for a precise number, **huh**? Okay, if you want to talk specifics, we can tell you that the average penis is 6 inches when erect (there's more on erections in the coming pages, but for now let's define an erection as a penis that's gone from soft and limp to hard and upright). In that upright position, most guys measure between $5\frac{1}{4}$ and $6\frac{3}{4}$ inches from the tip of their penis to its base where it meets their body.

Just remember, this average is only for an erect penis (and average means that lots of people are smaller and others bigger). When your penis is soft, or flaccid, it won't be **nearly** that large.

And here's where the issue gets really confusing. Some penises look a lot bigger in the soft position than others. But this **size difference** usually disappears when the penises are erect. In other words, a penis that appears big in the soft position will probably grow less than one that's on the small side in the soft position.

You should also know that your own soft penis size will vary **depending on the situation**. For example, if you're standing out in the cold, your penis will be smaller than if you're warm and inside. Whether you're feeling nervous or relaxed can also make a difference.

One final point: Your penis will continue to grow during the entire puberty process. In fact, a lot of guys are eighteen years old before theirs is fully-grown. So try not to make too many locker room comparisons, especially if you happen to be in there with some upperclassmen. Things will all even out in the end.

THE FACTS
ABOUT FORESKINS

Size may be the biggest issue boys have when it comes to the penis. But circumcision is not far behind. That's because a penis that's been circumcised looks different from one that hasn't.

Circumcision is an operation that removes the foreskin of the penis. It is a custom of many religions, including Judaism and Islam. But many boys from other religions are circumcised because some docs believe the procedure prevents disease. Other doctors dispute those claims, and argue that the operation is not as painless as once believed. Whether you're circumcised or uncircumcised, chances are there will be lots of other boys who look the same. **But just in case** you're not sure which group you fall in, here's a quick description of each:

CIRCUMCISED

The big difference with a circumcised penis is that the **foreskin has been removed**. As a result, you can see the entire glans of the penis. The **corona**, a ring around the bottom of the head of the penis, is visible as well. Boys who have been circumcised will have some kind of scar from the operation. Without the protection of the foreskin, the skin of the glans loses its moist, shiny feel.

UNCIRCUMCISED

On an uncircumcised penis, the foreskin is still intact. It covers the corona and most of the head like a hood. When boys are born, the foreskin can't be pulled back, or retracted. But as they get older, their foreskin separates slowly from the head of their penis. During puberty, the foreskin usually **retracts** enough that the entire head of the penis is visible. Sometimes this happens before puberty, and sometimes it happens after puberty. It's important to let the foreskin retract **naturally**. You never want to force it. If you're worried that the process is happening too slowly, speak with a trusted adult, or ask your doc about it the next time you go in for a checkup.

KEEPING IT CLEAN

Whether you're circumcised or not, it's important to keep your penis clean by **washing it daily**, preferably in the shower. This will prevent infection and also keep any odors in check. While your private parts don't produce the same body odor as your armpits, it can get pretty **smelly** down there if you go too many days without a wash. If you haven't been circumcised, pull back gently on the foreskin to rinse your glans. Soap can irritate the soft skin under the foreskin, so just clean the area with warm water instead.

WHAT'S LEFT BEHIND?

We've focused almost entirely on the front half of your private area. But there's also the backside. You shouldn't notice **too much change** with your rear, certainly nothing on the order of what's happening with the penis. **A few developments may occur, however**. For one, pubic hair may find its way from your genitals all the way to your buttocks and anus. Sweat glands in these areas can become active as well, causing additional wetness and odor around the anus. The best way to **combat odor** is to wipe the region thoroughly with toilet paper after you go to the bathroom. You also need to shower and change your underwear regularly, especially after playing sports or other sweaty activities.

THE TWO "E" WORDS

Up until now, we've been talking mainly about how your penis will change shape during puberty. But there's **a lot going on in the inside** of the penis, too. And these developments will alter your life even more than the appearance of pubic hair. With that, it's time to talk about the two "e" words: **erection** and **ejaculation**.

WHAT IS AN ERECTION?

You probably already know the answer to that. Erections start at a very young age. Even babies experience them. But once boys hit puberty, **erections** start to, well, spring up at a very rapid rate, and often when you least expect or want it—like in the middle of class, right before your teacher calls you up to the board!

An erection occurs when the penis fills with blood. It may feel like there's a bone in there, but the stiffness is nothing more than blood filling the erectile tissue in your penis. Some form of sexual stimulation often causes this, but the blood can start flowing for no reason at all. The rush of blood will usually cause the penis to turn a darker color.

The penis can go from **soft to hard** in a matter of seconds, or the process can take a few minutes. In general, the older you get, the longer it takes to reach a full erection. How long an erection lasts also decreases with age.

Erections take on a different curve and angle, so **don't be alarmed** if yours seems to be pointing in an odd direction. When the penis curves, it usually does so to the left. Angles are usually the same each time, so if yours sticks out straight now, it will probably always point that way.

DID YOU KNOW?

During puberty, the average male experiences six or seven erections each night while they sleep. Each erection will last anywhere from twenty to thirty minutes. That means you might have an erection for more than two hours during the course of the night!

THE TRUTH ABOUT EJACULATION

An ejaculation is when semen gets pumped through and out of the urethra, the tiny tube that runs through the middle of the penis. This is the same tube that urine travels through when it leaves your body. When the penis is about to ejaculate, a valve between the urethra and the bladder closes, which means you can't urinate and ejaculate at the same time.

Ejaculation is actually a two-stage process. The first stage is called **emission**. This is when sperm from the testicles gets mixed with other bodily fluids to create semen. Feelings of sexual arousal build very rapidly during this initial stage.

The second stage of ejaculation is called **expulsion**. This is when semen is pumped through the urethra and out the urethra opening by a series of intense muscle contractions. The liquid ranges in color from clear to gray to white with a tinge of yellow or orange. Sometimes, a couple of drops of sticky fluid will appear at the tip of the penis right before ejaculation. This is known as **pre-ejaculatory fluid**.

It usually takes **three or four strong contractions** to force all of the semen out of the penis. These will be followed by a series of smaller contractions, which may be accompanied by additional semen. It may feel like a ton of liquid is pouring out, but the average ejaculation contains only a teaspoon or so.

WET DREAMS

The medical term is nocturnal emission, but most people know it simply as a wet dream. Wet dreams are just like any waking ejaculation. Semen is discharged from the penis through the urethra, usually during a dream that features some type of sexual imagery and arousal. Guys may wake up in the middle of a wet dream. Or they may not know they had one until the morning, when the proof will be in semen-stained sheets or underwear.

Wet dreams can be a little **embarrassing**. Try not to worry about it. A lot of guys have wet dreams at one time in their life. If you're concerned about your sheets, either toss them in the hamper or rinse the stain with a wet paper towel. There's absolutely **nothing to be ashamed of**, but if you want to keep your wet dreams to yourself, **that's your business**.

PRIVATE PARTS
SMARTS

1. **True or False**

All boys start puberty at the same time.

2. **The average size of an erect penis is:**

A) 4 to 5 inches

B) 5 to 6 inches

C) 7 to 8 inches

D) 9 to 10 inches

3. **Small red bumps around the penis at the start of puberty are caused by:**

A) A skin rash

B) Sexual thoughts

C) Acne

D) Hair follicles poking the skin

4. The tool doctors use to measure testicle size is called a:

A) odometer

B) orchidometer

C) thermometer

D) pedometer

5. True or False

Men with large penises are better at sports.

GET A LEG UP

4

Your lower body is what gets you through the day—**literally transporting you from place to place**. It's made up of three basic parts: the thigh, the leg, and the foot. Within each part is a **complex system** of bones, muscles, joints, tendons, and more. During puberty, these parts are developing at a rapid pace. In fact, your legs (like your arms) often grow faster than your torso during puberty, which might mean a few months of **funny body proportion**, as your upper body catches up with your lower body. But fear not, it will all even out in time.

ON YOUR MARK, GET SET
GROW!

The puberty growth spurt takes place all over the body, but your lower half will be **especially busy** during the next few years. The average dude shoots up nine to eleven inches during puberty, and a lot of that spurt happens in his legs. The **so-called height spurt** usually happens earlier for girls, which is why many eleven- and twelve-year-old girls are a head taller than their male classmates—making for **super-awkward** slow dances at parties. But within a few years, boys usually catch up and surpass them.

Height is largely genetic, so if your parents are tall it's likely that you will be as well. But genes aren't the only factor. Maintaining a healthy diet and getting lots of sleep at night and exercise during the day will help your body reach its full potential.

STRAIGHT TALK

You've heard tall people are more successful. You're only average height, and that's with big boots on. Our culture does put a lot of importance on height. In movies, for example, the hero of the story often towers over the bad guys. In reality, however, many movie actors tend to be very short. It's more important to be comfortable with your personal height. Keep in mind that the average height of adult men in the U.S. is 5 feet 10 inches tall!

WHAT A PAIN! GOING THROUGH GROWING PAINS

You're lying in bed at night drifting off to sleep when all of a sudden an **intense spasm** of pain shoots up your leg. Welcome to your first (but probably not last, unfortunately) **growing pain**. They're common between the ages of eight and twelve, and usually occur in the **thighs**, **calves**, **or backs of the knees**. Painful as they are, growing pains usually don't require medical treatment. Doctors think they're probably the result of overtired muscles. If you have a very active day with lots of running, climbing, or jumping, be sure to **stretch your legs** before you go to bed. Applying a heating pad to sore muscles is another good way to prevent growing pains. If the soreness is **severe**, ask your mom and dad if you can take an over-the-counter pain reliever such as acetaminophen or ibuprofen.

STAYING OFF THE DISABLED LIST

Y ou have muscles throughout your body, even in your face. But the **muscles in your legs** get the most work, since they're used in walking, running, and other forms of movement. All that activity **increases the chance of injury**. Strains and sprains are the two most common. You can suffer either type of injury in other parts of your bod, but since they're most likely to affect your legs, we'll talk about them here.

WHAT'S THE DIFF?
STRAINS VS. SPRAINS

To understand the difference between these two injuries, you first need to know how the muscles in your body work. There are **three types of muscles**: **skeletal**, **smooth**, **and heart**. Skeletal muscles make up approximately forty percent of your body and are controlled voluntarily. Heart and smooth muscles are generally associated with your body's organs, and aren't under your conscious control.

Skeletal muscles regulate movement in your legs and other parts of the body. They attach to the bones in two places by a tough cord of tissue called a **tendon**. Nerves in the muscle receive messages from the brain telling it what to do: walk, run, kick, whatever. When the **brain sends a signal**, muscles contract and relax to make the body move. Sometimes, they stretch too far, causing tiny ruptures in the muscle tissue. **Suddenly you've got a strain**. You may not notice it right away, but within a few hours the pain, swelling, and stiffness to the muscle will definitely get your attention!

Strains can be painful, but they're not as serious as sprains. A sprain doesn't actually involve the muscle directly, but instead is caused by stretching or tearing the ligaments that hold bones together at the joints. Ankles and knees can sprain easily, especially during sports when it's easy to twist a joint or fall funny on it. The injured area will probably start to hurt right away, and you may have trouble walking.

Whether you suffer a strain or a sprain, **the most important thing is to stop moving right away**. You sometimes hear about athletes "playing through the pain." This might sound brave, but in fact it's just foolish, since it can turn a relatively harmless injury into something far more serious.

Get the injury checked out by a doctor or medical trainer. They'll check for swelling and tenderness, and may end up ordering an **X-ray** to make sure you didn't break a bone. If you have a sprain, you may need to wear a splint or temporary cast for three or four weeks. If it's a strain, you'll just need to rest the injury for about a week or so.

In addition to **rest**, apply **ice** to the injury and try to keep it **elevated** so that it's higher than your heart. This will decrease swelling. After twenty hours, you can **switch from ice to heat**, either from a warm compress or heating pad, to soothe the aching muscle.

"I'M AFRAID IT'S BROKEN"

No one wants to hear those words, let alone a busy teenager who might be in the middle of soccer or baseball season. But **broken bones are a fact of life**. Wearing protective equipment when you play sports will reduce the risk, but accidents happen. **There are several types of fractures**, the medical term for when a bone snaps under too much pressure. A **hairline fracture** is a tiny break that you may not even notice at first. An **open fracture** is when the bone breaks and sticks out of the skin (Yikes!).

Depending on the severity of break, your doctor may need to reconnect the bone with special pins. Or you may get away with just a brace or plaster cast. These devices are designed to keep the bone from moving so that it has time to put itself back together.

DID YOU KNOW?

You have 206 bones in your body. That's a lot of opportunity for breaks! The largest bone is the femur, or thighbone. The smallest is a tiny bone located in the middle of the ear.

BONE UP ON CALCIUM

Puberty is a very important time for bones. The hormones that are released into your body at this time help make bones thicker and stronger. **But hormones alone can't build up your bones.** You also need to take in plenty of minerals including **calcium** and **zinc**. Exercise is also essential for building up the bone mass. Besides strengthening your heart and muscles, it helps deposit calcium in the bones. Unfortunately, most teenage boys only get about half as much calcium as they should. Don't let that be you!

To give your bones the calcium they need to grow strong and healthy, you need to take in at least 1,300 milligrams of calcium each day. One 8-ounce glass of calcium-fortified milk contains about 300 milligrams. What if you don't exactly love guzzling a big glass of cow juice? No problem, there are loads of other foods that fit the bill.

Check out this chart on some surprising foods that are high in calcium:

8-oz container of plain, low-fat yogurt: 415 milligrams of calcium
3 oz of sardines: 325 mg
1.5 oz of cheddar cheese: 307 mg
a half cup of firm tofu: 204 mg
a half cup of instant hot chocolate: 53 mg
a half cup of spinach: 146 mg
a half cup of canned white beans: 96 mg

WHAT'S THAT SMELL?

Your feet are probably the hardest working parts of your body. They walk, they run, they kick, they dance, and more. Wherever you want to go, your feet take you there. In return, they get to spend the whole day crammed inside a pair of dirty, old sneakers. **Some thank you**! Seriously though, we ask a lot of our feet. One result of all the hard work they do is a whole lot of sweat.

Unlike other forms of sweat, foot sweat can't evaporate easily away from the body. The damp, dark interior of **sweaty shoes** is the ideal breeding ground for bacteria called **micrococcus sedentarius**. These bacteria feast on the dead skin cells and oils on your feet. The waste from these bacteria takes the form of a foul-smelling organic acid. **No wonder it smells so bad**!

Foot odor is only a serious problem for ten to fifteen percent of the population and can be controlled in most cases. The most important thing is to **clean your feet regularly** in the shower or bath. Get between the toes where bacteria like to hide. Dry thoroughly with a towel before putting on your socks. If your feet sweat a lot, you can wear special, moisture-absorbing socks. These tend to cost more than regular socks, but if they help with your foot odor problem, it's worth it. As for shoes, **try not to wear the same pair every day**. Putting them out in the sun can kill off bacteria. And don't wear shoes if they get too tight, since this causes the feet to sweat more.

If, after all this, your feet still **stink**, ask your mom or dad about disinfectant sprays or powders. A doctor can also prescribe special medicine to treat foot odor, but this should be a last resort.

ATHLETE'S FOOT: AN ALL-STAR IRRITATION

The name is a little misleading. You might be a terrible athlete and still get hit with this itchy fungus. The scientific name is **tinea pedis**, but it's called athlete's foot because it breeds in showers, locker rooms, and other places where athletes hang out. But it can strike anywhere. Seven in ten people will get it at some point in their lives, but it's most common among teenage guys. **So look out!**

The first sign of athlete's foot is dry, cracked skin on the bottom of your feet and between the toes. If left untreated, the fungus will spread to the rest of your feet, including your toenails. It will also turn red and raw from all the itching and scratching you're likely to do.

Many of the same rules that apply to preventing foot odor go for athlete's foot. Clean your feet regularly, dry thoroughly, and don't wear the same shoes and socks two days in a row. You also have to be extra careful in locker rooms by wearing sandals in the shower and using your own towel.

If you start to notice a rash, you can **stop it in its tracks** with antifungal powders and sprays. If these don't stop the itch, see your doc for a stronger medication.

BATTLING BLISTERS

Blisters are common among athletes, but you might experience one just by wearing a new pair of shoes. **Anything that rubs against the skin can result in a blister** by causing the top layer of skin to separate from the rest of your body. When this happens, the small pocket that's created beneath the top layer of skin fills with fluid. This is a blister.

You'll probably be tempted to **pop** the blister. But this can let germs to spread to the surrounding skin (the same way popping a pimple can lead to more pimples). Instead, **cover the blister with a bandage** and stop doing whatever it was that caused the rubbing in the first place. If the blister is big, or it doesn't go away on its own after a few days, you may want to see a doctor.

GET OFF ON THE RIGHT FOOT WITH THIS QUIZ

1. The average of height of men in the United States is:

A) 5 feet

B) 5 feet 10 inches

C) 6 feet

D) 6 feet 6 inches

2. True or False

Athlete's foot only happens if you play a lot of sports.

3. The best way to minimize foot odor is to:

A) Wash your feet regularly with soap and water.

B) Change your socks every day.

C) Air your shoes out in the sun.

D) All of the above.

4. Growing pains usually affect the following body part:

A) Muscles

B) Bones

C) Skin

D) Organs

5. Which of the following minerals is most important to developing strong bones:

A) Potassium

B) Calcium

C) Sodium

D) Magnesium

Answers:

1. B

2. False. This fungus is often spread in locker rooms, but anyone can catch it.

3. D

4. A

5. B

Up until now, this book has focused mainly on the physical changes that take place during puberty. But there's **an awful lot going on inside, too**. During puberty, it's actually normal to feel strange. In fact, it would only be strange if you didn't feel strange. Pretty . . . uh strange, huh? The point is that it's totally okay to feel out of sorts as your body goes through puberty's many changes. As hard as it might be at times, you need to **let yourself experience these feelings** and not lock them away or pretend they aren't happening.

Life is full of challenges. You've probably experienced some of them already. As you begin the transition into adulthood, these challenges will start to come faster and harder. Learning to meet them head-on is one of the most important lessons.

WHAT'S GOING ON IN THERE?

The entire puberty process starts with a **pea-shaped gland** at the base of the brain called the **pituitary** gland. Somewhere around the age of nine, the **pituitary**

begins secreting hormones, which causes other glands to release more hormones throughout the body. **Testosterone** is the most important of these other hormones. It's what causes just about everything discussed in this book, including pubic hair, acne, and all sorts of other stuff.

But testosterone and other hormones don't just affect you physically. They also change the way you think and feel. During puberty, you'll probably experience **emotions** that you've never felt before. Even if you've always been a happy guy, you might find yourself feeling sad or overly sensitive at times. Or you might lose your temper over stuff that never used to bother you. A lot of boys also grow apart from their parents and siblings, even

those who used to love nothing more than family time (don't worry—these feelings don't mean you don't love your family).

These emotional changes can be hard to handle. But it's really important to remember that they're largely the result of hormonal stuff happening inside your body. The human body is a pretty sophisticated piece of equipment, but it's not perfect. At times, it might release too much testosterone, causing **mood swings** and other emotional reactions. Eventually, your body will get the balance of hormones just right. Until then, remember that **puberty doesn't just happen to your body**. Your mind goes through it too.

TOUGH TRANSITION

The sense of confusion and awkwardness puberty brings isn't just about hormones. There's also the issue of your changing place in the world. Puberty is often described as **the bridge between childhood and adulthood**. That's a lot of ground to cover in a fairly short span of time.

Think about it. Before puberty begins, most kids are still in grade school, with not much to worry about beyond their homework and maybe a few chores. By the time they come out the other side, they might well be **driving a car**, **keeping a part-time job**, **and thinking about college**.

While you're in the middle of those **two extremes**, don't be surprised if you sometimes feel pulled in both directions. Most guys love the idea of being a grown-up, especially the **freedom** and **independence**. But adulthood also means a lot of hard work and **responsibility**, and that can be overwhelming.

Learning to manage this confusion is one of the trickiest parts of puberty. Sure, parents all went through puberty, too. But they're pretty far removed from the experience, so they may not remember exactly what it was like. This doesn't mean you shouldn't talk to your mom or dad about your feelings. It just means there will be times when you feel like **no one really understands what you're going through**.

So what can you do in those moments? If you don't want to talk to Mom or Dad, you can always turn to another trusted adult, such as a teacher, nurse, older sib, or religious leader. If you're unable to talk to another person, just **writing down your feelings in a journal** can be helpful. The important thing is to get them out of your head. If you let them fester too long in there, they'll only get worse.

ALL THE OTHER KIDS ARE GOING THROUGH PUBERTY FASTER THAN I AM

First of all, **that probably isn't true**. It only seems that way because you're becoming so much more aware of your body and everybody else's. It's **human nature** to see things in other people that we don't see in ourselves. One of the best examples of this is your voice changing (covered in Chapter 2). You probably won't notice your voice getting gradually deeper in the coming months. But you'll definitely be aware of it when some guy in your class sounds like Darth Vader.

Like we've said, the speed at which boys go through puberty varies. Boys that start early won't necessarily finish first! In fact, it may be a **late bloomer** who ends up sporting his first **'stache and burns** (also covered in Chapter 2) way before anyone else!

I'M NOT SURE WHO MY REAL FRIENDS ARE.

Puberty comes at a rough time. For a lot of guys, the intense physical change takes place during the transition to middle school, when they're also thrust into a brand-new social setting. And even if you don't change schools, you may find yourself **growing apart** from your old friends at this time. Either way, you'll probably have to make new buds amidst all the changes that are happening to your body. **Not cool**!

Friendship comes easier for some kids than for others. There's no magic formula for making friends, but there are things you can do to increase your chances. Here are the **three "Bs"** of successful friendship.

★ **Be friendly.** That might sound totally obvious, but being friendly is one of the most **important steps** to making friends. Having a warm smile and an energetic handshake will make people want to get to know you better. And that one quality will take you far. It's **not** that life is one big popularity contest. But the most successful people are often able to get along well with others. Now's the time to work on that skill!

★ **Be yourself.** This is another **key** to friendship. People can usually pick up on phony behavior pretty quickly, and it's a major turnoff. Then there's curiosity. By **asking a lot of questions** and coming up with new places to visit and things to do, you'll show the person that you're both interested and interesting.

★ **Be considerate.** Try to **head off** any disagreements before they turn into a full-fledged fight. **Miscommunication** can ruin any relationship, especially a friendship that's just getting off the ground. If it bothers you that your new bud is always borrowing your stuff, tell him how you feel before his borrowing gets out of hand. If the friendship is meant to be, he'll appreciate your honesty and try to be more sensitive in the future.

SOME KIDS IN MY SCHOOL ARE GETTING INTO THINGS THAT I'M NOT COOL WITH

Welcome to the world of **peer pressure**. For a lot of guys, this social challenge begins right around puberty (as if you didn't have enough to worry about already!). Resisting peer pressure can be difficult, especially if you're in a new school and want to be accepted by your classmates. But if you give in once, it will be **harder to say no** in the future. And in the wrong crowd, it doesn't take long for minor bad behavior to escalate into stuff that's either against the law or bad for your health and well-being.

That's why it's important to be prepared for peer pressure so that you're not caught off guard. Here are a few secret weapons:

⭐ **Self-confidence.** This is probably the best defense against peer pressure. It's like a muscle: **the more you practice self-confidence, the stronger it becomes**. Start by saying "no" to the relatively small stuff, like arriving late to class. Not only will this get you used to standing up for yourself, the kids doing the pressuring will realize you're not someone who goes along with the crowd. In fact, that may be enough to put an end to your peer pressure troubles.

⭐ **Avoidance.** Another way to avoid peer pressure is to, well, avoid it! Stay away from the kids who do it. That might be easier said than done—after all, you don't usually get to decide which students you sit next to in class. But you can always **remove yourself from potentially threatening situations**. For example, if you know kids might be smoking at an upcoming party, go to the movies instead.

⭐ **Alliances.** It's super-important to find at least one other friend who shares your position. Once you two find each other, chances are other kids will want to hang out with you as well. **That's the nice thing about peer pressure—it can be positive as well as negative**. The secret is to find a group of friends who will always push you in the right direction.

You're at a party where some members of the "cool" crowd are smoking and drinking. It's a good idea to have a special signal, such as a text message code ("What time is the party tomorrow?"), that you can send your parents to let them know you want to leave.

I'VE BEEN GETTING PICKED ON A LOT AT SCHOOL, AND SOMETIMES IT GETS PHYSICAL.

There's peer pressure, and then there's **bullying**. Neither one is any fun, but if you find yourself the victim of bullying, it's important to **talk to a trusted adult right away**. You might be tempted to fight back against a bully. But this really isn't the best response, since the situation can quickly escalate into a more serious form of violence.

It can be difficult to know the difference between peer pressure and bullying. In cartoons and TV, the school bully is usually easy to spot. He's the one with ripped jeans, a gruff voice, and long, messy hair. But in real life, bullies come in all shapes and sizes. Kids often become bullies at school because they are **insecure**. Or sometimes it's a result of a lot of physical and verbal abuse at home. It's definitely a **sad situation**, but it doesn't make it okay for them to pick on other kids.

Unfortunately, **bullying is extremely common**. In fact, three out of four kids say they've experienced it. This can lead to physical scrapes and bruises, as well as more serious emotional damage. Sometimes kids worry so much about bullying that they actually start to become physically sick. **There are a few strategies for keeping the bullies at bay**.

★ **Strategy 1:** **Steer clear**. Do your best to avoid a bully, even if it means taking a different route to and from school. It's not cowardly to avoid confrontation with a bully, since they're not the kind of people who respond well to reason. You're not going to convince a bully to stop picking on you, no matter how logical your argument might be, so it's better to steer clear of him.

⭐ Strategy 2: Ignore.

If you can't avoid a bully, do your best to ignore him (or her). Most bullies are looking to get a reaction from their victims. Acting indifferent to his threats or ridicule might be enough to make him go away.

⭐ Strategy 3: Stand up.

If avoidance and ignorance both fail, you may have no choice but to stand up to a bully. This can be terrifying, but effective. Rather than resorting to violence, shouting "No! Stop it!" is the best way to stand up to a bully. Ideally, you'll have the opportunity to do this when there are other kids around who will back you up in your protest. Most bullies have more than one victim, so there's a good chance you won't have to look too far for allies.

⭐ Strategy 4: Speak out.

If none of the techniques above work and someone is threatening you repeatedly, it's important to tell a parent or a teacher. This is by far the hardest thing to do. You may be worried about being called a snitch or a baby and suffering even worse bullying. But adults are here to help you when you can't resolve a problem alone. You may be surprised by the solutions they come up with!

THE OLDER I GET, THE LESS MY PARENTS SEEM TO UNDERSTAND ME.

So yeah, **parents and children argue a lot**. But the bickering does tend to hit a high point right around puberty. The reason for this is pretty simple: As boys make the transition into adulthood, they want to assert their **independence**. Most 'rents want this for their sons, but they often have a different idea about what it means to be independent.

Look at curfews. You might think you're old enough to stay out as late as you want. Because parents have been exposed to more of the world's dangers they'll probably insist you come home at an early hour. (For the record, the average **curfew** for thirteen-year-old boys is 9 P.M. on school nights and 10 P.M. on weekends.)

Learning to manage this parental conflict is one of the hardest parts of being a kid. It all comes down to trust.

Here are the building blocks:

⭐ **Responsibility.** If you can prove to your folks that you're responsible, say, by keeping your room clean and maintaining good grades, they'll **reward** you by granting you more freedom, like pushing your curfew back thirty minutes. **In the end, though, what they say goes while you are still a kid**. When you grow up, you'll be able to come home whenever you like.

⭐ **Communication.** This the other key to dealing with the 'rents. Because your parents are older, you might not think you can initiate a discussion with them. **But parents are usually open to hearing what their children have to say**, especially if it's obvious they've given the matter a lot of thought. Remember, parents really do want to see their kids grow into mature adults!

KEEPING A CHECK ON SIBLING RIVALRY

If you have sisters and brothers, puberty may put some additional strain on the relationships. **Younger sibs** will probably want to hang around even more now that they see you becoming an independent adult. Older siblings **might be a little freaked** with the fact that their baby bro is turning into a man right before their eyes (if it's an older brother, he might even feel a little threatened).

Families sure are complicated! But it's okay to have mixed feelings about your sibs. Some days you might love them, and some days you might wish they lived in another country. The important thing to remember is that your **siblings will be with you throughout your entire life**. Even if you fight like cats and dogs now, chances are the relationship will evolve as you all get older. And when it comes to managing the 'rents, there's no better ally than a sister or brother.

111

Still, there are bound to be times when **nothing** seems to tame the sibling rivalry. During those moments, it's important to have a small part of the home that's just for you. **The sense of privacy** will calm you down during any of puberty's difficult moments, especially those involving a pesky sister or brother.

I'M A LOT MORE EMOTIONAL THAN I'VE EVER BEEN

The extra hormones in your body are likely to cause frequent mood swings during puberty. So don't be surprised if a seemingly insignificant event—such as a lower-than-expected grade on a test or an argument with a sibling—sends you on an **emotional rollercoaster**. It's all part of the process. But there are things you can do to minimize the mood swings.

★ **Eat right.** People get irritable when they're **hungry**, so try not to skip meals, especially breakfast. Your mind and body need to fuel up in the morning.

★ **Get enough sleep.** Being **overtired** not only makes you sluggish, it can also make you cranky. You should try to get ten hours of sleep each night.

★ **Stay active.** Exercise is a great way to release stress and emotional energy that might otherwise eat you up inside. If you're not into sports, look for another form of exercise—such as **playing catch with your dog** that will get your blood moving a few times a week.

★ **Go with the feelings.** Emotions are a huge part of who we are as individuals. You need to take the good with the bad. That includes anger, sadness, jealousy, and other negative emotions. The important thing is that you **learn from these emotions**. Ask yourself later why you got mad at a certain friend, or why it depresses you to see the adults in your life argue. Once you've processed your feelings, **move on**. While it's important to be in touch with your emotions, you don't want to dwell on them.

THE ABC'S OF ZZZ'S

So just how much sleep do you need at this time in your life? If you're twelve or younger, experts say you should get approximately **ten hours each night**. That might sound like a lot, but sleep is really important for the body as well as for the mind.

You probably know the grogginess that comes with getting too little sleep the night before. What you may not realize is that your **brain is actually working more slowly, too**. If you have a big test that day, chances are you won't do as well as if you did get the amount that doctors recommend. Your **immune system** (which defends your body against illness) is also affected by sleep, so too many late-night horror movie marathons are bound to result in a case of the sniffles or other sickness.

HERE ARE FIVE QUICK TIPS FOR GETTING A GOOD NIGHT'S SLEEP

1: Set a consistent bedtime.
This will help your body get into the routine of falling asleep. Try to wake up at the same time too. It's okay to reward yourself with an extra hour or so on the weekends.

2: Stay away from stimulants.
It's never a good idea to drink beverages with a lot of caffeine, including soda and coffee. But after 4 P.M., it's a definite no-no, since these stimulants can work on the brain for many hours.

3: Don't keep a TV in your room.
Studies prove that kids with a TV near their bed sleep less. Reading before bed is a much better way to unwind.

4: Get plenty of exercise.

Late afternoon is the best time to give the body a workout. Don't exercise right before bedtime, since it will take a while for you to come down from the adrenaline rush.

5: Make it cozy.

A dark, cool environment ups your chances for a good night's sleep. If you're afraid of being chilly, throw an extra blanket onto the bed.

DID YOU KNOW?

Tears are a way for the body to get rid of chemicals that build up during times of emotional stress when you're feeling sad or angry. This is where the expression "cry it out" comes from—you're actually crying out the bad chemicals that come from these feelings. Some guys are embarrassed to cry because they think it makes them less of a man. But all they're doing is hurting their bodies, and that really will make them less of a man!

I FEEL STRESSED OUT ALL THE TIME

There's more going on in your life than ever before. It's only natural to get a little overwhelmed at times. But there's a limit. If you're having trouble sleeping or concentrating at school, you may be headed toward **stress overload**. There's a right way and a wrong way to deal with your stress. **Follow this list of dos and don'ts:**

DO

Talk it out. Whether with a close friend or a trusted adult, talking about your problems always helps manage them.

Work it off. Exercise is great for the body, but it can do wonders for your mind as well. Getting the blood moving will release tension and boost your energy.

Have a laugh. There's nothing like a good joke to chase your stress away. Watch a comedy or hang with a friend who always makes you crack up.

Log off. It's a 24/7 world out there. Sometimes you need to turn off the laptop and cell phone and recharge your own internal battery.

DON'T

Eat your troubles away.
It can be tempting to find comfort in junk food. But studies prove that a healthy diet has a calming effect on the body.

Lose your temper. It's okay to express anger when the feelings are justified. But yelling and screaming just for the sake of it won't solve your problems.

Ignore the situation. Stress won't go away if you pretend it isn't there. Facing your issues head-on is the best way to overcome them.

Take on even more. It's okay to want to please your parents, teachers, coaches, and friends. But you always need to prioritize your needs first, or you won't be any good to those around you.

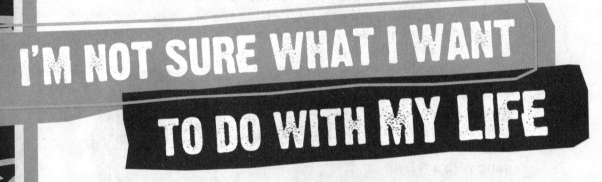

I'M NOT SURE WHAT I WANT TO DO WITH MY LIFE

That's ok, you don't have to be sure! There are the rare cases where so-and-so knew he wanted to be a doctor or an actor or a scientist at the age of four. But most people are young adults before they figure out their **true calling**.

It's important to **try as many different things as possible** right now. This has several benefits. It will let you figure out what you're really good at. It will expose you to all different types of people. And it will help make you a **well-rounded** dude, on his way to becoming a dynamic, multitalented adult.

HERE'S A LIST OF FIFTEEN THINGS EVERY TEEN SHOULD DO ONCE.

You may not get to everything on the list. But even if you only hit half of the activities, you'll discover new passions and talents—and have lots of fun in the process.

Play an instrument. Listening to music is one thing. Knowing how to create it is another. There are dozens of instruments to choose from, so if you don't like the first one you pick up, try another. Even banging on a bongo can be very satisfying.

Hit a fastball. You don't have to try out for the baseball team. Putting the bat on the ball at a batting cage is enough to experience this awesome feeling.

Learn to cook. Food is one of the greatest pleasures in life. Learning to cook will expose you to all its many flavors—plus it's a great way to impress friends (especially girlfriends!). Start with something simple, like spaghetti with meat sauce or homemade chocolate chip cookies.

Learn CPR. You're never too young to save a life. Talk to your health teacher or school nurse about taking a course.

Tie a necktie. Every guy should know how to do this fundamental act of dressing. Plus a tie is a great way to add a bit of color and style to an outfit.

Shine a pair of shoes. Like tying a necktie, being able to shine your own shoes is one of the necessary skills of every sharp-dressed man.

Dance. There are going to be lots of chances to dance in your life. Don't be shy!

Catch a fish. There's something so satisfying about pulling a live fish from a running stream. It's also a great way to get into nature. Throw the fish back into the water if you don't want to eat it for dinner.

Change a tire. This is one of those things everyone should know how to do. Ask an older person in your life, such as a dad, aunt, or brother.

Snap a portrait. Seeing the world through a camera lens will give you a whole new perspective. Remember to ask permission when photographing strangers.

Throw a spiral. It might not make you the star of the football team. But being able to throw a football will come in handy throughout your life, from flag football games at family reunions to passing around the pigskin at the beach.

Start a journal. A journal is an excellent place to get thoughts and feelings out of your head and onto the page or to do some creative writing like poems or stories.

Learn a foreign language. Your school probably requires this one. But try not to think of it as schoolwork. Foreign languages are windows into other cultures.

Make a movie. Borrow a video camera, write a script, and cast the parts using kids in the neighborhood. Steven Spielberg made his first movie when he was a kid, and now he's one of the most successful directors in the world.

Volunteer in your community. You might hear that this looks great on your college application. That might be true. But it also just feels really good.

ARE YOU READY FOR THE UPS AND DOWNS OF PUBERTY?

TAKE THIS POP QUIZ

TO FIND OUT?

1. Most thirteen-year-old boys have to be home at what time on a weekend?

A) 9 o'clock

B) 10 o'clock

C) 11 o'clock

D) Whenever they darn well please!

2. True or False

It's okay to like some subjects in school more than others.

3. The recommended number of hours of sleep for pre-teenage boys is

A) 7 hours

B) 8 hours

C) 9 hours

D) 10 hours

4. What gland in the body is responsible for hormones?

A) The pituitary gland

B) The mammary gland

C) The thyroid gland

D) The salivary gland

5. True or False

Peer pressure is always negative.

CONCLUSION:

OK, so you know that puberty can make you feel frustrated, awkward, or confused at times, but you also know that it's an exciting step in growing up. Everything you're going through is completely normal and you are definitely not alone. So, remember to take care of yourself (mentally and physically), seek out help when you need it, focus on the positive, and try to enjoy the ride. And for the moments when you have questions and want some extra help, this guide will be there.

INDEX: